Jesus Loves You Because...

And Some Things He Likes Too!

Fulton Books, Inc.
Meadville, PA

Published by Fulton Books 2021

ISBN 978-1-63985-548-3 (hardcover)
ISBN 978-1-63985-549-0 (digital)

Printed in the United States of America

Jesus Loves You Because...

And Some Things He Likes Too!

By Ampa Jensen

Illustrated By Aubrie Waltman

This book is dedicated to my wife Debbie, my daughters Melissa and Jennifer, my son-in-law Ric and my grandkids Mav, Milo, and Olivia. Also, every single adult who takes the time to teach children about the mysterious, unfathomable love of God.

A.J.

Dear Parent,

With the single exception of Jesus Himself, we know more about King David than any other biblical character. This is no coincidence when we consider that David is called "a man after God's own heart" (1 Sam. 13:14). God even says, "Behold, I have made him a pattern to the peoples" (Isa. 55:4).

Intimacy with God is obvious in David's poems and reflections on his life. Even with his rather impulsive lifestyle, limited Old Testament perspective, and no physical encounter with God, David truly trusted Him. He honored and loved God—because David truly knew God.

Most Christian children's literature misses the significance of this core truth: God IS LOVE. We know we cannot earn our way to heaven, yet many adults struggle as we compare our own relationship with God to others'. We may measure ourselves against those we feel are good (or bad) Christians. We may keep mental lists of our good deeds against what we do wrong.

Yet that is not how a loving God sees us. And this was also not David's understanding of who God is. David knew that God IS LOVE. Therefore he could trust God at every moment, with every problem, amidst every failure, and despite any sin. David always ran back to the arms of God, his safe place, the only place of eternal restoration and perfect relationship.

This little book is intended to be a tool for parents. It is meant to counter voices that tell our children that Jesus/God only loves you if you behave well. That single message damages our kiddos. The harm is deeply engrained. It becomes a problem in adulthood when we begin to wrestle with our identity and our relationship with God. We may ask, "Am I good enough," "How can God love me," or "Why would God ever forgive me when I...?"

Does Jesus "like it" when we behave well? Of course. We were created to show God's love to others. Yet our activities are secondary to the model given in scripture. Like David, we should first be men and women "after God's own heart." What motivated David's love affair with our Creator? That secret is explored in this book.

The secret is that we are not teaching our kids to obsess over behaviors that Jesus "likes." Instead, let's train them to pay close attention to their relationship with God. Let's launch them on an intentional journey that underscores "WHY JESUS LOVES" each one of us.

Sincerely,

Ampa Jensen

Jesus <u>likes</u> <u>it</u> when you forgive.

1

2

But Jesus <u>loves</u> <u>you</u>
because you are His kiddo.

"But to all who did receive Him, who
believed in His name, He gave the
right to become children of God."
—John 1:12

Jesus <u>likes</u> it
when you share.

6

But Jesus <u>loves</u> <u>you</u> because
you are a part of His story!
We were created for God's glory and honor! —Isaiah 43:7

Jesus <u>likes</u> <u>it</u>
when you pray.

But Jesus <u>loves</u> <u>you</u>
because He knows you
and how you feel.

God, you know my thoughts.
—Psalms 139: 1 and 2

Jesus <u>likes</u> it when you gather with the church family!

13

But Jesus <u>loves</u> <u>you</u>
because He knows
everything about you!

God knows the number
of hairs on our head!
—Luke 12:7

Jesus <u>likes</u> <u>it</u> when you share Him with friends and make Him a part of your life.

17

18

But Jesus <u>loves</u> <u>you</u>
because He not only died
for you, He died with you!

When Jesus died so He could be
raised from the dead forever,
He shared His death with you
so you can live forever.
—Galatians 2:20

20

Jesus <u>likes</u> it when you obey your parents.

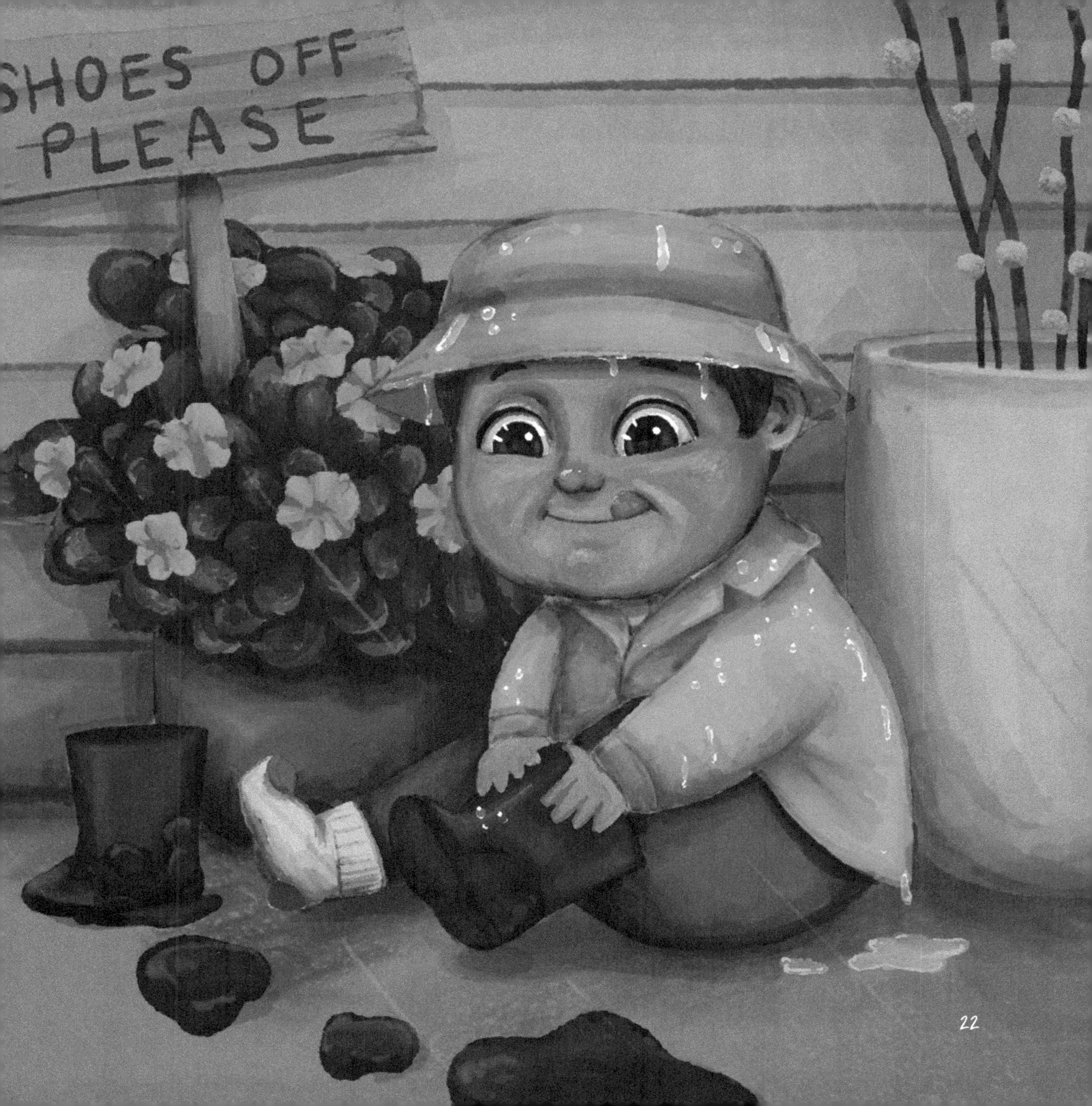
SHOES OFF
PLEASE

But Jesus **loves** _you_ because
Jesus loves everyone!

"neither height nor depth, nor anything else in all creation, will be able to separate us from the love of God that is in Christ Jesus our Lord."
—Romans 8:39

Jesus likes it when

you tell the truth.

But Jesus <u>loves</u> <u>you</u> because
you are more important
than anything to Him.

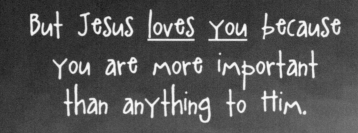

"For God so loved the world that
He gave His one and only Son, that
whoever believes in Him shall not
perish but have eternal life."
—John 3:16

28

Jesus <u>likes</u> <u>it</u> when you say you're sorry.

30

But Jesus <u>loves</u> <u>you</u> because you have always been a part of His plan.

God has had plans for our lives for His reasons, not ours, before time began. —2 Timothy 1:9

Jesus <u>likes</u> <u>it</u> when you're kind.

But Jesus <u>loves</u> <u>you</u>
because He loves families
and you can be a part
of His forever family.

See how much the Father God loves us, He calls
us His children because that is what we are.
—1 John 3:1

36

Jesus <u>likes</u> <u>it</u> when you listen
to stories about Him.

But Jesus <u>loves</u> you
because He made you to
be with Him and share
His home in Heaven.

Jesus said that I go to Heaven to
prepare a place for you so that
where I am, you can be also.
—John 14:2

Jesus <u>loves</u> <u>you</u>
because He
wants to live in
and with you!

Do you know that if you invite
God to live with you, then the
spirit of God lives in you?
—1 Corinthians 3:16

Jesus <u>loves</u> <u>you</u>
because He is
glorified by you.

"I am the Lord Your God everyone
who I created for MY glory and
who I formed and made."
—Isaiah 43: 1 through 7

45

Jesus loves you
because He is love!

"God is love."

—1 John 4:8

Always remember,
Jesus loves you

48

CPSIA information can be obtained
at www.ICGtesting.com
Printed in the USA
BVHW021045130222
R13147800001B/R131478PG628404BVX00001B/1

9 781639 855483